D0251445

Potato Salad

Potato Salad

65 Recipes from Classic to Cool

Debbie Moose

Photography by Jason Wyche

John Wiley & Sons, Inc.

This book is printed on acid-free paper. ♾

Published by John Wiley & Sons, Inc., Hoboken, New Jersey
Published simultaneously in Canada

For general information on our other products and services or for technical support, please contact our Customer Care Department within the United States at (800) 762-2974, outside the United States at (317) 572-3993 or fax (317) 572-4002.

Wiley also publishes its books in a variety of electronic formats. Some content that appears in print may not be available in electronic books.
For more information about Wiley products, visit our web site at www.wiley.com.

PROP STYLING BY LESLIE SIEGEL
FOOD STYLING BY JAIME KIMM
BOOK DESIGN BY DEBORAH KERNER

LIBRARY OF CONGRESS CATALOGING-IN-PUBLICATION DATA:
Moose, Debbie.
Potato salad : recipes from classic to cool / by Debbie Moose ; photography by Jason Wyche.
p. cm.
Includes index.
ISBN 978-0-470-28348-6 (cloth)
1. Cookery (Potatoes) 2. Salads. I. Title.
TX803.P8M658 2009
641.6'521–dc22
2008027970

Printed in China

10 9 8 7 6 5 4 3 2 1

To Rob,

my little sweet potato.

Contents

Acknowledgments

Thanks to all my "tater tasters" for this book:
Anthony Nance, Shelly Kramer, and the other stylists of The Elan Group; my husband's coworkers at Scenera Research; the famished features department of the *News & Observer* (Raleigh, North Carolina); the Literary Lovelies; and friends and neighbors.

I'd also like to thank those who contributed favorite recipes for the book:
Cathy Hedberg, Carol Reuss, Liz Biro, Linda Naylor, Sheri Green, Maggie Kellum Chalk, the U.S. Potato Board, and Kurt and Ruth Muller.

I offer a big thank-you to Justin Schwartz, my editor at Wiley, who makes me look good.

A special thank-you to chefs and cookbook authors who graciously allowed me to include their fabulous recipes: Alicia Ross, Beverly Mills, Ben Barker, Robin Robertson, Lucy Saunders, and Stephanie Tyson.

For their advice and support, huge hugs of gratitude to Elizabeth Swaringen, Jean Anderson, and my hardworking agent Carla Glasser, as well as to my colleagues of the Association of Food Journalists.

And to Martha Waggoner, the person who started the potato salad madness, I hope I used enough celery.

Root Issues

My friend Martha loves potato salad. She's very particular about it, insisting that celery must be included—to her, it's as important as the spuds themselves. Over lunch one day, she spent most of an hour dissecting potato salads served at various neighborhood eateries and finding most of them below her standards.

Honestly, I had never given potato salad much thought before then. But on mulling it over, I realized it's not just a starchy buddy to the hamburger. Potato salad comes in many cultural guises, from the Russian appetizer to the oil-and-vinegar-and-bacon German dish, to the dill-accented Scandinavian delight. And, of course, it's the all-American side dish at every Fourth of July picnic. But this great dish deserves to shine year-round, not just during the summer—it is truly a salad for all seasons.

In this book are the flavors of beloved favorites. Some traditional salads get new twists. Many recipes bring in international touches, reflecting the popularity of potato salad around the world. A chapter of main-dish salads will make it easy to feed a crowd with one bowl.

So, make potato salad a melting pot of influences from around the world. Take it to stardom by adding meats and even caviar. Go spud wild. I think even finicky Martha would approve, as long as you don't leave out the celery.

More than two hundred varieties of potato have been developed over the centuries, going all the way back to the 1500s, when Peruvians cultivated the vegetable in a rainbow of colors. But a potato is just a potato, right? Not when it comes to making potato salad. There are two basic types of potatoes: waxy and mealy (also called starchy). Waxy varieties, such as some fingerlings, purples, round reds, round whites, and many yellow potatoes, are the best for boiling and for use in potato salad. They are lower in starch and will hold their shape. Mealy potatoes, which include Idahos and russets, have higher starch content and are better for other uses, such as baking and mashing.

New potatoes—small potatoes that appear in the spring—are not a variety of their own, but can be of any type. The key is that they are small and freshly dug: hence the moniker *new*. New potatoes are moist and sweet, and do not hold up for long storage the way other potatoes do. Like the spring in which they appear, they are short-lived. New potatoes are fabulous for potato salads and rarely even need peeling. You may also see them called creamers.

Sweet potatoes, deep orange and full of healthy beta-carotene, have a natural sweetness and a lot of moisture. Paired with the right ingredients, they make potato salads that are unusual in flavor and hue.

WHICH POTATOES TO PICK?

I have suggested varieties for each recipe in this book. But except for the recipes using sweet potatoes, you may substitute any of the waxy types of potato that you prefer. My personal favorites are new potatoes, small reds, and Yukon Golds. I prefer to peel the Yukon Golds and use those for recipes where I want to cut the potatoes in small pieces for a finer texture.

New potatoes and many tender waxy varieties of potato don't require peeling. Their peel is very soft, and it can add a rustic color to the salad. You will need to peel if you choose to dice the potatoes rather than cutting them into rough chunks or quarters.

PREPARING POTATOES

The traditional way to prepare potatoes for salad is to boil them. Use plenty of water. Cover the pot with a lid and the potatoes will come to a boil faster, plus you'll have less steam in your kitchen. Some cooks peel and cut up the potatoes before boiling. That method saves some time, but you run the risk of the cut potatoes absorbing too much water during cooking, giving your salad a mushy texture. Boiling the potatoes whole, unpeeled, eliminates that threat.

OK, I can hear some of you saying that your Mama always used Idahos and cut them into tiny pieces before boiling them, and she made the best potato salad on Earth. If that is true, I wouldn't dare tamper with a Mama's sainted recipe. If you have a method that works for you, go with it. But try my suggestions if you're a potato salad novice.

For a change, abandon the pot and try roasting or grilling the potatoes. You'll find interesting differences in texture, and with grilling, you'll get a smoky flavor as well. Roast the potatoes, either whole or in chunks, in a nonstick pan at 400°F. To grill, cut the peeled potatoes into ½-inch slices, use an oiled grill pan to prevent them from slipping through the grate, and turn frequently with long-handled tongs or a spatula.

While some potato salads can be eaten immediately, the flavors of most improve with at least a few hours' mellowing time. For best food safety, store salads made with mayonnaise or sour cream in the refrigerator immediately after preparation, and get them cooled down fast. If you're taking the potato salad to an outdoor picnic, be sure to keep it cold while serving. Carry it in a well-iced cooler, and serve from a bowl nestled in a larger bowl or tray of ice. Use all potato salads, whether mayo-based or not, within about two days of preparing or the quality may decline, as the spuds become soft and fall apart.

SERVING POTATO SALAD

Color and appearance is important in serving potato salad. Dress it up in a colorful bowl or platter, garnish with extra ingredients such as parsley or relish, or use decoratively cut curls of carrot or radish, if you're adept with a knife.

For the recipes in this book, I used regular mayonnaise and sour cream. However, if you really want to use reduced- or low-fat versions, those will work too. I always go for the fat and bacon, but I do recognize that others don't share that enlightened approach to life.

Prefer more salt? Like dill pickle relish instead of sweet? Follow your potato salad muse! The beauty of potato salad is that you don't have to be too exact about it. Some of the best recipes aren't written down. Rustic chunks of potato often look better than obsessively cut cubes. Start with the recipes I offer and make a homey, comforting potato salad that is your family's own.

PICNIC PALS

SERVES 6

Farmer's Market Salad

A springtime stroll through my local farmer's market inspired this recipe. Be sure to use small new potatoes, about the size of a Ping-Pong ball or a golf ball. To prevent any possibility of curdling, wait until the potatoes and peas are near room temperature before adding the dressing.

2 pounds new potatoes
½ cup cooked peas
¼ cup chopped sweet onions (such as Vidalia, OSO Sweet, or Texas 1050)
1 hard-cooked large egg, chopped
¼ cup chopped celery
½ cup sour cream
1 tablespoon mayonnaise
1 teaspoon fresh lemon juice
½ teaspoon freshly ground black pepper
½ teaspoon salt
2 tablespoons chopped fresh Italian parsley
1 teaspoon chopped fresh chives

Place the potatoes in a large pot, add enough water to cover them, cover the pot with a lid, and bring to a boil. Cook until the potatoes are pierced easily with the tip of a sharp knife, 15 to 20 minutes. Drain and let cool until you can handle them. Cut into quarters or halves, depending on the size of the potatoes.

In a large bowl, toss together the potatoes, peas, onions, egg, and celery. In a small bowl, combine the sour cream, mayonnaise, lemon juice, black pepper, and salt. Pour the dressing over the vegetables, add the parsley and chives, and toss well to combine. Cover and refrigerate for several hours to overnight.

SERVES 6

Potato Salad Olé

The Mexican flavors of this spicy and creamy salad go well with everything from grilled chicken to meat loaf.

2 pounds red potatoes, quartered but not peeled
½ cup chopped onions
1 teaspoon chopped garlic
3 tablespoons canned chopped green chiles, drained
1 tablespoon chili powder
1 teaspoon dried oregano
½ teaspoon ground cumin
1 cup sour cream
1 teaspoon salt
1 teaspoon freshly ground black pepper
1 teaspoon fresh lime juice
2 tablespoons chopped fresh cilantro (optional)

Preheat the oven to 425°F. Spray a baking pan with nonstick cooking spray. Put the potatoes in the pan. Roast for 30 to 40 minutes or until the potatoes are pierced easily with the tip of a sharp knife. Cool to lukewarm.

In a large bowl, stir together the onions, garlic, green chiles, chili powder, oregano, cumin, sour cream, salt, black pepper, and lime juice. Add the potatoes and toss until coated. Cover and refrigerate for several hours to overnight.

SERVES 6

Herbs and Garlic Salad

Fresh colors and flavors make this potato salad a great match for lighter meals.

2 pounds Yukon Gold potatoes
1 teaspoon chopped garlic
¼ cup chopped fresh Italian parsley
2 tablespoons chopped chives
½ cup chopped onion
1 cup mayonnaise
1 tablespoon Dijon mustard
½ cup chopped celery
½ teaspoon salt
½ teaspoon freshly ground black pepper
1 teaspoon dried thyme

Place the potatoes in a large pot, add enough water to cover them, cover the pot with a lid, and bring to a boil. Cook until the potatoes are pierced easily with the tip of a sharp knife, 15 to 20 minutes. Drain and let cool until you can handle them but they are still warm. Peel and cut into approximately 1-inch pieces.

In a large bowl, stir together the garlic, parsley, chives, onion, mayonnaise, Dijon mustard, celery, salt, and black pepper. Crush the thyme lightly with your fingers and stir it in. Add the potatoes and toss until coated. Cover and refrigerate for several hours to overnight.

SERVES 6

Saucy Salad

This salad, with the flavor of sweet-tangy barbecue sauce, would be great alongside burgers and hot dogs. I used a North Carolina barbecue sauce called Thomas Sauce, but select any slightly sweet and not-too-thick sauce that you prefer.

- 2 pounds Yukon Gold potatoes
- ½ cup barbecue sauce
- ½ cup chopped onions
- ½ cup chopped celery
- ½ cup mayonnaise
- 1 teaspoon chili powder
- ½ teaspoon chopped garlic
- ½ teaspoon salt
- ½ teaspoon freshly ground black pepper
- 1 teaspoon apple cider vinegar
- 2 tablespoons chopped fresh Italian parsley

Place the potatoes in a large pot, add enough water to cover them, cover the pot with a lid, and bring to a boil. Cook until the potatoes are pierced easily with the tip of a sharp knife, 15 to 20 minutes. Drain and let cool until you can handle them but they are still warm. Peel and cut into approximately 1-inch pieces.

In a large bowl, stir together the barbecue sauce, onions, celery, mayonnaise, chili powder, garlic, salt, black pepper, and apple cider vinegar. Add the potatoes and toss until coated. Cover and refrigerate for several hours to overnight. When ready to serve, sprinkle the parsley on top.

SERVES 6

Ranch House Potato Salad

This easy side dish uses ranch dressing and simple additions to create a potato salad that tastes like you worked all day on it. The dressing contains salt, so you may not need more; taste and see.

2 pounds white potatoes
1 cup ranch dressing
¾ cup chopped red onion
¾ cup chopped celery
¼ cup chopped fresh Italian parsley
¼ cup crumbled cooked bacon
½ teaspoon freshly ground black pepper
Salt to taste

Place the potatoes in a large pot, add enough water to cover them, cover the pot with a lid, and bring to a boil. Cook until the potatoes are pierced easily with the tip of a sharp knife, 15 to 20 minutes. Drain and let cool until you can handle them but they are still warm. Peel and cut into approximately 1-inch pieces.

In a large bowl, combine the ranch dressing, red onion, celery, parsley, bacon, and black pepper. Taste, then add salt, if needed. Stir in the potatoes. Cover and refrigerate for several hours to overnight.

SERVES 10 TO 15

Cheryl's Tangy Mustard Potato Salad

My friend Sheri Green in Raleigh, North Carolina, who is a great cook, got this recipe from her niece. It is definitely for mustard lovers. You can halve or double the recipe easily. Reduced-fat mayo works in this recipe, but don't use the fat-free version. And refrigerating the salad overnight is key to the flavor—don't rush it!

10 pounds potatoes
3 tablespoons salt, or to taste
2 cups mayonnaise
¾ cup yellow mustard
1 (10-ounce) jar dill cubes or dill relish, undrained
Freshly ground black pepper to taste
1 large yellow onion, ends and outer skin removed

Place the potatoes in a large pot, add enough water to cover them, cover the pot with a lid, and bring to a boil. Cook until the potatoes are pierced easily with the tip of a sharp knife, 15 to 20 minutes. Drain and let cool until you can handle them but they are still warm. Peel and cut into 1- to 2-inch pieces.

Place the potatoes and salt in a very large mixing bowl. Combine thoroughly. Add the mayonnaise, mustard, dill cubes with their juice, and pepper. Stir together thoroughly and set aside.

Cut the onion in half, widthwise, and gently score the top of each half. Place the halves in the bottom of a serving dish, scored sides facing up. Place the potato salad on top of the onion halves. Cover and refrigerate overnight.

SERVES 6 TO 8

Grilled Potato Salad

Lucy Saunders loves to find creative ways to cook with great beers, and this salad will keep people talking at the cookout. The recipe is from her cookbook *Grilling With Beer: Bastes, BBQ Sauces, Mops, Marinades and More, Made with Craft Beer* (F&B Communications, 2007). And there's more at www.grillingwithbeer.com.

⅓ cup canola oil
⅓ cup amber ale
3 ounces light cream cheese
1 teaspoon caraway seeds
½ teaspoon celery seeds
1 teaspoon brown mustard seeds
1 teaspoon salt
¼ teaspoon red pepper flakes
2 tablespoons minced fresh Italian parsley
2 pounds small red potatoes
2 tablespoons olive oil
1 cup chopped celery
½ cup English cucumber, peeled and sliced
3 scallions, minced (include some of the green tops)
⅓ cup dill pickle relish
⅓ cup chopped daikon radish
Salt and freshly ground black pepper to taste

Place the canola oil, ale, cream cheese, caraway seeds, celery seeds, mustard seeds, 1 teaspoon salt, red pepper flakes, and parsley in the container of a blender. Blend at high speed until the mixture is smooth. Refrigerate for at least 1 hour.

Prepare a gas or charcoal grill for indirect cooking. Toss the potatoes with the olive oil. Grill the potatoes until they are tender, turning often to prevent burning.

continues on p. 28

Remove from the heat, and when cool enough to handle, chop into bite-size pieces.

In a large bowl, combine the potatoes, celery, cucumber, scallions, dill pickle relish, and daikon radish. Add the dressing and mix well. Taste, then add salt and pepper if needed.

SERVES 6

Sweet Potato Waldorf Salad

Fruit pairs well with sweet potatoes, and this twist on the traditional Waldorf has a lighter flavor because it has no mayonnaise. Roasting the sweet potatoes provides a drier texture and more concentrated flavor, but boil them if you prefer.

2 pounds sweet potatoes
1 cup chopped Granny Smith apple, unpeeled
½ cup chopped celery
¼ cup chopped scallions
½ cup coarsely chopped walnuts
½ cup olive oil
¼ cup fresh lemon juice
Salt to taste
Freshly ground black pepper to taste
⅛ teaspoon cinnamon

Preheat the oven to 400°F. Prick the sweet potatoes with a fork and place on a baking sheet or in a roasting pan. Roast the sweet potatoes for about an hour, or until a fork pierces them easily but they are not mushy. Cool until you can handle them. Peel and cut into approximately 1-inch cubes and place in a large bowl.

Stir in the apples, celery, scallions, and walnuts. In a separate bowl, whisk together the olive oil, lemon juice, salt, pepper, and cinnamon. Pour the dressing over the potato mixture and toss. Cover and let sit at room temperature 2 hours before serving. Serve at room temperature.

SERVES 6

Interns' Potato Salad

The staff, volunteers, and student interns at Interact in Raleigh work twenty-four hours a day to help women and children who are victims of domestic violence and sexual assault. I feel privileged to volunteer with them. And they all like good food, too. The idea for this recipe came from one of the interns—I'm embarrassed to say I forgot which one, so I'll dedicate it to all of them.

- 2 pounds Yukon Gold potatoes
- ½ cup halved pimiento-stuffed green olives
- ½ cup chopped scallions
- ½ cup grated carrot
- 2 tablespoons dill pickle relish, drained
- 1 cup mayonnaise
- ¼ cup yellow mustard
- ½ teaspoon salt
- ½ teaspoon freshly ground black pepper

Place the potatoes in a large pot, add enough water to cover them, cover the pot with a lid, and bring to a boil. Cook until the potatoes are pierced easily with the tip of a sharp knife, 15 to 20 minutes. Drain and let cool until you can handle them but they are still warm. Cut into chunks.

In a large bowl, combine the olives, scallions, carrot, dill pickle relish, mayonnaise, mustard, salt, and pepper. Add the potatoes and stir to combine. Cover and refrigerate for several hours to overnight.

SERVES 8–10

Kellum Family Potato Salad

Maggie Kellum Chalk of Morehead City, North Carolina, got this dish from her mother, but the dressing recipe goes back to her grandmother. Maggie says that the no-mayo dressing allows the family to take the salad on boat rides or car trips without worry. Maggie's recipe was published in *A Little Taste of Heaven Since 1857: The Morehead City Heritage Cookbook*, which was produced for the coastal city's 150th anniversary in 2007.

1 can condensed tomato soup, undiluted
⅔ cup cider vinegar
¾ cup vegetable oil
1 tablespoon salt
2 tablespoons yellow mustard
1 large clove garlic
5 pounds red potatoes
3 cups chopped celery
1½ cups diced scallions
½ cup minced fresh Italian parsley
Crumbled cooked bacon for garnish

In a clean quart glass jar, combine the tomato soup, cider vinegar, vegetable oil, salt, yellow mustard, and garlic. Cover with the lid, shake well, and allow to sit overnight at room temperature for the flavors to blend.

Cut the potatoes into 1- to 1½-inch cubes, but do not peel. Put the potatoes in a large pot, add enough water to cover them, and bring to a boil. Boil until tender when pierced with a sharp knife, about 15 minutes.

Place the potatoes in a large bowl and pour the dressing over them. Cover and let sit overnight. Turn the potatoes with a spoon occasionally to coat them with the dressing.

When ready to serve, add the celery, scallions, and parsley; stir to combine. Top with crumbled bacon.

SERVES 6

Double Tater Salad

Combine new and sweet potatoes with smoked paprika and sweet raisins for an unusual salad that will keep 'em guessing. The sweet potatoes will take longer to cook than the new potatoes. Remove the new potatoes from the water with a slotted spoon or tongs as they are done.

1 pound new potatoes
1 pound sweet potatoes
¼ cup golden raisins
¼ cup sliced almonds
¾ cup olive oil
¼ cup apple cider vinegar
½ teaspoon smoked paprika
¼ teaspoon salt
1 teaspoon crushed dried red pepper
1 tablespoon Old Bay seafood seasoning

Place the potatoes in a large pot, add enough water to cover them, cover the pot with a lid, and bring to a boil. Cook until the potatoes are pierced easily with the tip of a sharp knife, 15 to 20 minutes. Drain and let cool until you can handle them but they are still warm. Cut the new potatoes into quarters or halves, depending on the size of the potatoes. Peel and cut the sweet potatoes into pieces of similar size.

In a large bowl, toss together the potatoes, raisins, and almonds. In a small bowl, whisk together the olive oil, vinegar, smoked paprika, salt, red pepper, and Old Bay. Pour the dressing over the potato mixture and toss to coat. Cover and let sit at room temperature 2 hours and serve, or refrigerate for several hours to overnight. Bring to room temperature before serving.

SERVES 6

PCPS (Pimiento Cheese Potato Salad)

My husband picked up the idea for this salad from someone who works in his building. I love pimiento cheese and gave it a twist by adding some heat. This salad would be great with any kind of picnic food, from grilled burgers to fried chicken.

2 pounds Yukon Gold potatoes
¾ cup chopped red onion
¾ cup chopped celery
1 tablespoon chopped pickled jalapeños
1 cup (7-ounce container) prepared pimiento cheese spread

Place the potatoes in a large pot, add enough water to cover them, cover the pot with a lid, and bring to a boil. Cook until the potatoes are pierced easily with the tip of a sharp knife, 15 to 20 minutes. Drain and let cool until you can handle them. Peel and cut into 1- to 1½-inch chunks. Let the potatoes cool to room temperature while preparing the other ingredients.

In a large bowl, combine the red onion, celery, and chopped pickled jalapeños. Add the potatoes and toss to combine. Add the pimiento cheese spread and stir until well mixed. Cover and refrigerate for several hours to overnight.

SERVES 6

Honey Mustard Salad

Make this flavorful side dish quickly by using prepared salad dressing. Radishes may seem like an unusual addition to a potato salad, but their peppery bite provides a nice contrast to the sweet dressing.

2 pounds Yukon Gold potatoes
1 cup chopped onion
1 cup chopped celery
¾ cup chopped radishes
¾ cup creamy honey mustard salad dressing

Place the potatoes in a large pot, add enough water to cover them, cover the pot with a lid, and bring to a boil. Cook until the potatoes are pierced easily with the tip of a sharp knife, 15 to 20 minutes. Drain and let cool until you can handle them. Peel and cut into 1- to 1½-inch chunks.

In a large bowl, combine the potatoes, onion, celery, and radishes. Stir in the salad dressing. Cover and refrigerate for several hours to overnight.

SERVES 6

Pesto Potatoes

Pesto has become almost as common a condiment as ketchup, and it gives a blast of flavor to this salad without a lot of work. It's like a good pasta salad, but heartier.

2 pounds Yukon Gold potatoes
¾ cup prepared pesto
¾ cup chopped rehydrated sun-dried tomatoes
½ cup chopped red onion
¾ teaspoon salt
3 tablespoons olive oil
2 tablespoons drained capers

Place the potatoes in a large pot, add enough water to cover them, cover the pot with a lid, and bring to a boil. Cook until the potatoes are pierced easily with the tip of a sharp knife, 15 to 20 minutes. Drain and let cool until you can handle them. Peel and cut into 1- to 1½-inch pieces.

In a large bowl, combine the pesto, sun-dried tomatoes, red onion, salt, olive oil, and capers. Stir in the potatoes. Cover and let sit at room temperature 2 hours or refrigerate overnight. Serve at room temperature.

SERVES 6

Ultimate Olive Salad

"Love the olives!" my tasters said. The strong flavors of the two kinds of olives balance well with the mild taste of the potatoes. Try this one with grilled or roasted chicken.

2 pounds Yukon Gold potatoes
¾ cup halved pimiento-stuffed green olives
½ cup pitted and halved Kalamata olives
¼ cup chopped red onion
¾ cup chopped fresh Italian parsley
1 cup mayonnaise
1 teaspoon Dijon mustard
½ teaspoon salt
½ teaspoon freshly ground black pepper
½ teaspoon dried oregano or marjoram

Place the potatoes in a large pot, add enough water to cover them, cover the pot with a lid, and bring to a boil. Cook until the potatoes are pierced easily with the tip of a sharp knife, 15 to 20 minutes. Drain and let cool until you can handle them. Peel and cut into 1- to 1½-inch pieces.

In a large bowl, toss together the potatoes, olives, onion, and parsley. In a separate small bowl, stir together the mayonnaise, Dijon mustard, salt, pepper, and oregano or marjoram. Pour the dressing over the vegetables and stir to coat. Cover and refrigerate for several hours to overnight.

SERVES 6

Lemony Dill Salad

The tart flavors of this salad make it a perfect match with rich foods or, as a friend and I discovered, spicy-hot chicken wings while watching a basketball tournament on television.

- 2 pounds Yukon Gold potatoes
- 1 cup chopped celery
- ⅓ cup chopped fresh Italian parsley
- ⅔ cup sour cream
- ⅓ cup mayonnaise
- ½ teaspoon chopped garlic
- 2 teaspoons fresh lemon juice
- 1 teaspoon finely grated lemon zest
- 1 teaspoon salt
- 1 teaspoon freshly ground black pepper
- 2 tablespoons dill pickle cubes
- Chopped fresh dill for garnish (optional)

Place the potatoes in a large pot, add enough water to cover them, cover the pot with a lid, and bring to a boil. Cook until the potatoes are pierced easily with the tip of a sharp knife, 15 to 20 minutes. Drain and let cool until you can handle them. Peel and cut into 1- to 1½-inch pieces.

In a large bowl, toss the potatoes, celery, and parsley. In a small bowl, stir together the sour cream, mayonnaise, garlic, lemon juice, lemon zest, salt, black pepper, and dill pickle cubes. Pour the dressing mixture over the vegetables and stir to coat. Cover and refrigerate for several hours to overnight. When ready to serve, garnish with fresh dill, if desired.

SERVES 8 TO 10

Sweet Potato Salad

Chef Ben Barker of Magnolia Grill in Durham, North Carolina, says that even people who claim to hate sweet potatoes love this salad. Ben uses a homemade pepper relish, but you can use a commercial one. The recipe is from *Not Afraid of Flavor: Recipes from Magnolia Grill,* by Ben and Karen Barker (University of North Carolina Press, 2000).

2 pounds sweet potatoes, peeled and cut into ½-inch chunks
1 cup Pickled Pepper Relish with juice (recipe follows)
1 teaspoon minced garlic
2 tablespoons Dijon mustard
¼ cup olive oil
Salt to taste
Freshly ground black pepper to taste
Worcestershire sauce to taste
¼ cup chopped fresh Italian parsley

Cook the sweet potatoes in salted water until done but still firm. Plunge them in ice water to stop them from cooking and drain well.

Combine the relish, garlic, and Dijon mustard in a bowl. Whisk in the olive oil, as well as salt, pepper, and Worcestershire sauce to taste.

Fold in the sweet potatoes and Italian parsley and toss gently. Keeps refrigerated for 2 days. Serve at room temperature.

MAKES 2 PINTS

Pickled Pepper Relish

- 1 cup green bell pepper, seeded, stemmed, and cut into small dice
- 1½ cups red bell pepper, seeded, stemmed and cut into small dice
- 1 medium red onion, cut into small dice
- 6 ounces cider vinegar
- 3 ounces sugar
- 1½ teaspoons salt
- ½ teaspoon celery seed
- 2 dried chipotles, halved and seeded (optional)

Place the vegetables in a 2-quart nonreactive pot. Pour in enough boiling water to cover the vegetables and let stand for 10 minutes. Drain.

Add the vinegar, sugar, salt, celery seed, and chipotles, if desired, to the vegetables. Bring to a boil and then simmer over low heat for 15 minutes.

To can the relish, ladle it into 2 hot pint jars and fill to within ¼ inch of the rim. Wipe the rim, seal the lids, and process in a boiling water bath for 15 minutes. Start timing after the water bath reaches full boil. Check to be sure the jars are securely sealed. The relish will keep for up to 6 months.

If you prefer to skip the canning, this relish can be refrigerated for up to 3 months, covered, in clean, sterile containers. This recipe can be scaled up easily, but be cautious with the chipotles.

SERVES 6

Tahini Treat

A creamy salad dressing flavored with the sesame paste called tahini, plus garlic and lemon, is a favorite of mine. I've made the dressing from scratch, but now it's on supermarket shelves, making it quick and easy to flavor a potato salad. It's sometimes called lemon tahini or tahini goddess dressing; look for tahini in the ingredients list if you're not sure. The dressing is a great sauce for sautéed greens or steamed asparagus, too.

2 pounds new potatoes
⅓ cup chopped fresh Italian parsley
½ cup chopped onion
½ cup chopped red bell pepper
¾ cup tahini salad dressing
Salt and freshly ground black pepper to taste
Chopped fresh chives for garnish (optional)

Place the potatoes in a large pot, add enough water to cover them, cover the pot with a lid, and bring to a boil. Cook until the potatoes are pierced easily with the tip of a sharp knife, 15 to 20 minutes. Drain and let cool until you can handle them. Cut into quarters or halves, depending on the size of the potatoes.

In a large bowl, toss together the potatoes, parsley, onion, and red bell pepper. Pour the dressing over the vegetables and toss to coat. Taste, then add salt and pepper, if needed. Cover and refrigerate for several hours to overnight. When ready to serve, garnish with chives, if desired.

German Warm Potato Salad

This recipe from Kurt and Ruth Muller of Pittsboro, North Carolina, is the fruit of their German heritage. The dish is a favorite at Fearrington Village University of Carolina at Chapel Hill Alumni Club. Use the smaller amount of apple cider vinegar and beef stock if using the smaller number of potatoes; the larger number for the larger amount of 'taters.

6 to 8 boiling potatoes
¼ pound bacon, diced
1 medium onion, minced
½ to ¾ cup apple cider vinegar
½ to ¾ cup beef stock
Salt and white pepper to taste
Minced fresh Italian parsley for garnish

Place the potatoes in a large pot, add enough salted water to cover them, cover the pot with a lid, and bring to a boil. Cook until the potatoes are pierced easily with the tip of a sharp knife, 15 to 20 minutes. Remove the potatoes from the heat, cool, peel, and cut into thick slices, and place in a large serving bowl. Set aside.

Stir together the vinegar and beef stock; set aside.

In a separate pan, fry the bacon over medium heat until golden, and remove it from the pan to drain on paper towels. Add the onion to the bacon drippings and cook, stirring, over medium heat until the onions are transparent, 5 to 6 minutes. Remove the pan from the heat and pour in the vinegar and beef stock. Taste, then add salt, if needed, and a large pinch of white pepper. Return the pan to the heat and bring to a boil.

Crumble the bacon over the potatoes. Pour the vinegar mixture over the potatoes and bacon, folding everything together gently. Sprinkle with minced parsley. Serve warm.

SERVES 6

Quick Italian Salad

My tasters loved the creamy texture of this salad—and how easy it is to make. The bell peppers echo the colors of the Italian flag.

2 pounds new potatoes
½ cup chopped green bell pepper
½ cup chopped onion
½ cup chopped red bell pepper
⅔ cup mayonnaise
⅓ cup sour cream
1 (0.6-ounce) package dry Italian salad dressing mix
Salt and freshly ground black pepper to taste
1 tablespoon each chopped green and red bell pepper, for garnish (optional)

Place the potatoes in a large pot, add enough water to cover them, cover the pot with a lid, and bring to a boil. Cook until the potatoes are pierced easily with the tip of a sharp knife, 15 to 20 minutes. Drain and let cool until you can handle them. Cut into quarters or halves, depending on the size of the potatoes.

In a large bowl, toss together the potatoes, green bell pepper, onion, and red bell pepper.
In a small bowl, stir together the mayonnaise, sour cream, and Italian salad dressing mix. Taste, then add salt and pepper if needed. Pour the dressing over the vegetables and toss to coat. Cover and refrigerate for several hours to overnight. When ready to serve, garnish with the additional red and green bell peppers, if desired.

SERVES 6

Triple-Cheese Potatoes

You may think there's bacon in this salad, but it's really the flavor of the smoked Gouda. For easy grating, make sure the Gouda is cold; it will be too soft at room temperature. "This tastes just like a twice-baked potato," one of my tasters said.

2 pounds new potatoes
¾ cup grated cheddar cheese
¾ cup grated Parmesan cheese
1 cup grated smoked Gouda cheese
⅔ cup mayonnaise
⅓ cup sour cream
2 teaspoons white wine vinegar
½ cup chopped celery
½ teaspoon salt
½ teaspoon freshly ground black pepper
1 tablespoon canned chopped pimientos, drained, for garnish (optional)

Place the potatoes in a large pot, add enough water to cover them, cover the pot with a lid, and bring to a boil. Cook until the potatoes are pierced easily with the tip of a sharp knife, 15 to 20 minutes. Drain and let cool until you can handle them. Cut into quarters or halves, depending on the size of the potatoes.

In a large bowl, combine the cheeses, mayonnaise, sour cream, white wine vinegar, celery, salt, and pepper. Stir in the potatoes. Cover and refrigerate for several hours to overnight. When ready to serve, sprinkle on the chopped pimientos, if desired.

SERVES 6

Classic Potato Salad

"This salad lives up to its name—a true classic!" said one of my tasters. This recipe will ring all your traditional potato salad chimes.

2 pounds new potatoes
⅓ cup chopped green bell pepper
⅓ cup chopped onion
3 hard-cooked large eggs, chopped
⅔ cup mayonnaise
1 teaspoon celery seed
2 tablespoons sweet pickle relish
2 tablespoons juice from pickle relish
Pinch of sugar
¾ teaspoon salt
1 teaspoon cider vinegar
1 teaspoon dry mustard
1 large dash cayenne pepper

Place the potatoes in a large pot, add enough water to cover them, cover the pot with a lid, and bring to a boil. Cook until the potatoes are pierced easily with the tip of a sharp knife, 15 to 20 minutes. Drain and let cool until you can handle them. Cut into quarters or halves, depending on the size of the potatoes.

In a large bowl, toss together the potatoes, green bell pepper, onion, and eggs. In a small bowl, whisk together the mayonnaise, celery seed, sweet pickle relish, relish juice, sugar, salt, cider vinegar, mustard, and cayenne. Pour the dressing over the potato mixture and toss to coat. Cover and refrigerate for several hours to overnight.

SERVES 4 TO 6

Close to Mom's Potato Salad

This dish has all the great taste of a classic potato salad, but because it uses soy mayonnaise, it's suitable for vegans or anyone who wants to get more healthy soy into their diet. You can purchase soy mayo, but it's not hard to make your own. Excerpted from *Vegan Planet* by Robin Robertson (Harvard Common Press, 2003).

1½ pounds red or white waxy potatoes
1 inner celery rib, minced
2 tablespoons grated onion
¼ cup sliced pimiento-stuffed green olives
¾ cup Soy Mayonnaise (recipe follows)
1 tablespoon white wine vinegar
1 teaspoon Dijon mustard
Salt and freshly ground black pepper
Paprika

Place the potatoes in a large saucepan with salted water to cover. Bring to a boil over medium-high heat and continue to boil until tender, about 30 minutes. Drain and allow to cool.

Peel the potatoes, cut into bite-size chunks, and place in a large serving bowl. Add the celery, onion, and olives and set aside.

In a small bowl, combine the soy mayonnaise, vinegar, mustard, and salt and pepper to taste. Mix well and add to the potato mixture, stirring gently to combine. Sprinkle the top with paprika. Serve right away or cover and refrigerate until ready to serve. This is best eaten within a day or two of being made.

MAKES ABOUT 1 CUP

Mayonnaise

- 6 ounces firm silken tofu, drained
- 1½ teaspoons white wine vinegar
- ¼ teaspoon dry mustard
- ½ teaspoon salt
- Pinch of sugar (optional)
- 3 tablespoons corn oil or other neutral-tasting oil

Place the tofu, vinegar, mustard, salt, and sugar, if using, in a food processor or blender and process until smooth. With the machine running, slowly add the corn oil in a thin stream through the feed tube until it is incorporated. Taste and adjust the seasonings. Transfer to a glass jar or other container with a tight-fitting lid. Cover and refrigerate until ready to use, up to 5 days.

SERVES 6

Roasted Potatoes with Mustard Vinaigrette

Two kinds of mustard give zing to the dressing for this salad. And because it's a vinaigrette, there will be no fear of mayo at your picnic.

- 2 pounds new potatoes
- 1 cup sliced spring onions
- ½ cup olive oil
- ¼ cup fresh lemon juice
- 1 teaspoon balsamic vinegar
- 1½ teaspoons Dijon mustard
- 1½ teaspoons Creole mustard
- 2 teaspoons chopped garlic
- 1 teaspoon salt
- ¼ teaspoon crushed dried red pepper
- ½ cup chopped fresh Italian parsley
- 3 tablespoons chopped fresh oregano

Preheat the oven to 400°F. Cut the potatoes into similarly sized pieces and place in a nonstick roasting pan. Roast for 30 to 40 minutes, or until the potatoes are pierced easily with a sharp knife. Place the potatoes in a large bowl and toss with the spring onions.

In a small bowl, whisk together the olive oil, lemon juice, balsamic vinegar, Dijon mustard, Creole mustard, garlic, salt, and red pepper. Stir in the parsley and oregano. Pour the dressing over the vegetables and toss to coat. Cover and let sit at room temperature 2 hours and serve, or refrigerate for several hours to overnight. Serve at room temperature.

SERVES 6

Sassy Salsa Salad

Use your favorite salsa to flavor this potato salad. It can be served right away, but it's even more flavorful if you can allow it to sit two hours.

2 pounds new potatoes
¼ cup chopped celery
¼ cup chopped red onion
1 cup salsa
1 teaspoon fresh lime juice
½ teaspoon chili powder
½ teaspoon chopped pickled or fresh jalapeños (optional)

Place the potatoes in a large pot, add enough water to cover them, cover the pot with a lid, and bring to a boil. Cook until the potatoes are pierced easily with the tip of a sharp knife, 15 to 20 minutes. Drain and let cool until you can handle them. Cut into quarters or halves, depending on the size of the potatoes.

In a large bowl, toss together the potatoes, celery, and red onion. In a small bowl, stir together the salsa, lime juice, chili powder, and jalapeños, if using. Pour the dressing over the vegetables and toss to coat. Cover and let sit at room temperature 2 hours and serve, or refrigerate for several hours to overnight. Serve at room temperature.

UPTOWN TATERS

SERVES 8

Smoky Bacon Salad

Bacon, potatoes, and fresh spinach add up to a salad with hearty flavors. Serve this alongside a good beef roast or grilled steaks.

3 pounds yellow fingerling potatoes
½ cup olive oil
⅓ cup apple cider vinegar
½ teaspoon salt
½ teaspoon pepper
2 cups coarsely shredded fresh spinach
1 cup chopped scallions
1 cup chopped fresh Italian parsley
¾ cup chopped cooked bacon

Place the potatoes in a large pot, add enough water to cover them, cover the pot with a lid, and bring to a boil. Cook until the potatoes are pierced easily with the tip of a sharp knife, 15 to 20 minutes. Drain and let cool until you can handle them but they are still warm.

In a small bowl, stir together the olive oil, apple cider vinegar, salt, and pepper.

Cut the potatoes in half and place in a large bowl. Toss the potatoes with the dressing, then toss in the spinach, scallions, parsley, and bacon. Serve immediately, warm or at room temperature.

SERVES 6

Rosemary-Roasted Garlic Fingerlings

When you have a rosemary bush as large as mine, you look for different ways to use the herb. Rosemary and garlic are a heavenly combination.

3 pounds yellow fingerling potatoes
¼ of a medium-size onion
1 head garlic
1 cup olive oil, plus more for drizzling
¼ cup white wine vinegar
2 tablespoons finely chopped fresh rosemary
1 teaspoon freshly ground black pepper
1 teaspoon salt

Preheat the oven to 400°F. Place the potatoes and onion on a nonstick baking pan. Place the head of garlic on a sheet of aluminum foil, drizzle with olive oil, and wrap tightly. Place the potatoes, onion, and garlic in the oven and bake for 30 minutes, or until the potatoes are pierced easily with the tip of a sharp knife.

Let the potatoes cool until you can handle them, then peel and slice into about ½-inch slices. Coarsely chop the onion. Place the potatoes and the onion in a large bowl.

Squeeze the garlic cloves into a small bowl, discarding the skins, and mash with a fork. Add 1 cup olive oil, white wine vinegar, rosemary, pepper, and salt. Stir well to combine. Pour the dressing over the potatoes and toss to mix well. Let sit at room temperature for 30 minutes to 1 hour before serving. Serve at room temperature.

SERVES 8 TO 10

Denise's Vinaigrette Potatoes with Asparagus

My friends Alicia Ross and Beverly Mills write the column "Desperation Dinners," which shows busy people how to feed their families quickly and well. They can also throw a party in a snap, and they tell the rest of us how in *Desperation Entertaining! Company's Coming: How to Make a Marvelous Meal in a Matter of Minutes* (Workman Publishing, 2002). This recipe from the book brings eye appeal as well as great flavor to the table.

2½ pounds small to medium-size red potatoes
1 pound fresh asparagus
3 scallions, chopped (about ½ cup, white and green parts)
Garlic-Dijon Vinaigrette (recipe follows)
2 tablespoons fresh Italian parsley
2 (2½-ounce) cans sliced black olives

Scrub the potatoes (leave the skins on) and place them in a 4½ quart Dutch oven or soup pot. Add just enough cold water to cover the potatoes. Cover the pot and bring to a boil over high heat. Once boiling, uncover and boil the potatoes until tender, about 20 minutes.

Meanwhile, snap the tough ends off the asparagus where they naturally break and discard the ends. Rinse the asparagus spears and cut into 1-inch pieces. Place in a single layer in a shallow, microwave-safe bowl and microwave, uncovered, on high just until crisp-tender,

2 to 3 minutes, depending on the thickness of the pieces, stopping halfway to rotate the bowl if necessary. When done, put the asparagus in a colander to drain and throw in 2 handfuls of ice cubes. Rinse with cold running water and toss gently with the ice cubes to stop the asparagus from cooking, about 1 minutes. Drain well, removing any unmelted ice cubes.

Rinse and finely chop the scallions.

Make the Garlic-Dijon Vinaigrette.

When the potatoes are done, put them in the colander to drain and throw in 2 handfuls of ice cubes. Rinse with cold running water and toss with the ice cubes until cool enough to handle. Drain well, removing any unmelted ice cubes, then cut the potatoes into ¼-inch slices and place in a large serving bowl. Pour the vinaigrette over the potatoes and toss to coat. The potato salad can be prepared to this point up to 24 hours ahead. Refrigerate the dressed potatoes, cooked asparagus, and chopped scallions, covered, separately.

Rinse the parsley well and shake to remove any excess water. Mince the parsley and add it to the bowl with the potatoes. Add the cooked asparagus to the bowl. Drain the black olives and add them to the bowl. Toss well to mix. The salad can be refrigerated, covered, at this point for up to 8 hours. Up to 30 minutes before serving, toss in the chopped scallions.

MAKES ABOUT 1 CUP

Garlic-Dijon Vinaigrette

- 4 cloves garlic
- ¼ cup red wine vinegar
- 2 teaspoons Dijon mustard
- ¼ teaspoon salt
- ¼ teaspoon freshly ground black pepper
- ¾ cup extra virgin olive oil

Drop the garlic cloves one at a time through the feed tube of a food processor with the machine running and finely chop.

Stop the machine and add the vinegar, mustard, salt, and pepper. Process to blend, about 5 seconds. With the motor running, drizzle the olive oil through the feed tube in a thin stream. Process just until well combined.

Note: The vinaigrette can be refrigerated, covered, for up to 3 days. Bring to room temperature, and whisk or shake well just before serving.

SERVES 6

Ginger Sweets

My home state of North Carolina is the nation's No. 1 producer of sweet potatoes, and we love 'em here. The flavor and color elevate this salad from a picnic treat to an elegant side dish. It's a different way to offer sweet potatoes on the Thanksgiving table, too.

2 pounds sweet potatoes
1½ teaspoons finely chopped fresh ginger
½ cup vegetable oil
⅓ cup orange juice
1 teaspoon fresh lemon juice
¼ cup finely chopped onion
¼ teaspoon finely chopped garlic
1 teaspoon salt
½ teaspoon freshly ground black pepper

Place the sweet potatoes in a large pot, add enough water to cover them, cover with a lid, and bring to a boil. Cook until the potatoes are easily pierced in the center with a sharp knife, 20 to 30 minutes. The cooking time will depend on the size of the potatoes.

While the potatoes are cooking, prepare the dressing. In a large bowl, whisk together the ginger, oil, orange juice, lemon juice, onion, garlic, salt, and pepper. Set aside.

Drain and cool the potatoes until you can handle them. Peel and cut into 1-inch cubes.

While the potatoes are still warm, add them to the bowl with the dressing and toss to combine (your clean hands are good for this). Cover and refrigerate for several hours to overnight. Serve at room temperature.

SERVES 6

Sweet Potato Ambrosia Salad

The sweetness of pineapple and dried cranberries blends with the natural flavor of sweet potatoes to make this salad. "It's a really unusual potato salad, but it's really good," one of my tasters said. Try it with roasted or grilled pork.

2 pounds sweet potatoes
½ cup mayonnaise
½ cup sour cream
2 teaspoons orange juice
½ teaspoon cinnamon
½ teaspoon salt
½ teaspoon freshly ground black pepper
¼ teaspoon sugar
½ cup dried cranberries
½ cup coarsely chopped pecans
½ cup canned pineapple chunks, drained
2 tablespoons coarsely chopped pecans for garnish (optional)

Preheat the oven to 400°F. Roast the sweet potatoes for about 1 hour, or until just tender when pierced with a fork. Do not overcook. Cool the potatoes until you can handle them, then peel and cut into approximately 1-inch chunks.

In a large bowl, stir together the mayonnaise, sour cream, orange juice, cinnamon, salt, black pepper, and sugar until well combined. Stir in the cranberries, pecans, pineapple chunks, and chopped sweet potatoes. Stir to coat everything with the dressing mixture. Cover and refrigerate for several hours or overnight. When ready to serve, garnish with chopped pecans, if desired.

SERVES 6

Tart Lemon Pepper Salad

This is a lemony potato salad—but I like tart flavors! If you have no time to refrigerate, just let the salad sit at room temperature for about 2 hours and stir it occasionally. It tastes best at room temperature.

- 2 pounds Yukon Gold potatoes
- 3 teaspoons lemon pepper seasoning
- 2 tablespoons dill pickle cubes, drained
- ½ cup chopped celery
- ½ cup chopped onion
- 2 tablespoons chopped fresh Italian parsley
- 1 hard-cooked large egg, chopped
- ¼ cup lemon juice
- ⅓ cup olive oil
- Salt and freshly ground black pepper to taste

Place the potatoes in a large pot, add enough water to cover, cover the pot with a lid, and bring to a boil. Cook until the potatoes are pierced easily with the tip of a sharp knife, 15 to 20 minutes. Drain and let cool until you can handle them but they are still warm. Peel and cut into approximately 1-inch pieces.

In a large bowl, toss together the potatoes, lemon pepper, dill pickle cubes, celery, onion, parsley, and hard-cooked egg. In a small bowl, whisk together the lemon juice and olive oil, then stir the mixture into the other ingredients. Taste, then add salt and black pepper, if needed. Cover and let sit 2 hours, or refrigerate for several hours to overnight. Serve at room temperature.

SERVES 8

Potato, Corn, and Cherry Tomato Salad with Basil Dressing

This salad captures the spirit of summer, with its fresh basil and just-picked vegetables. My friend Carol Reuss in Pittsboro, North Carolina, got the recipe from a neighbor, Cynthia Jones.

2 tablespoons white wine vinegar
½ cup olive oil
1 packed cup fresh basil leaves
Salt and freshly ground black pepper to taste
2½ pounds red potatoes
½ pound cherry tomatoes, halved
6 ears fresh corn, cooked, kernels removed

Put the white wine vinegar, olive oil, basil leaves, salt, and black pepper in a blender or food processor. Process until the mixture is emulsified.

Place the potatoes in a large pot, add enough water to cover them, and bring to a boil. Cook until the potatoes are pierced easily with the tip of a sharp knife, 15 to 20 minutes. Drain and let cool until you can handle them but they are still warm. Cut into quarters, but do not peel.

Put the potatoes, cherry tomatoes, and corn kernels in a large bowl. Pour in the basil dressing and toss gently to combine. Serve immediately.

SERVES 6

Curry Potato Salad

The flavors of Indian cuisine make a spicy, unusual spud salad. Using frozen peas is OK—just cook according to the package directions. And regular, low-fat, or fat-free yogurt will do fine.

2 pounds Yukon Gold potatoes
2 cups plain yogurt
3 cloves garlic, pressed
3 tablespoons Major Grey chutney
1½ teaspoons salt
1 tablespoon plus 1 teaspoon curry powder
1 cup cooked green peas
1 cup chopped onions
¼ teaspoon cayenne pepper, optional

Place the potatoes in a large pot, add enough water to cover them, cover the pot with a lid, and bring to a boil. Cook until the potatoes are pierced easily with the tip of a sharp knife, 15 to 20 minutes. Drain and let cool until you can handle them but they are still warm. Peel and cut into approximately 1-inch pieces.

In a large bowl, stir together the yogurt, garlic, chutney, salt, curry powder, green peas, onions, and cayenne pepper, if using. Stir in the potatoes. Cover and refrigerate for several hours or overnight.

SERVES 6

Tuscan Taters

Sun-dried tomatoes, capers, and basil give this potato salad the flavors of Italy. To reconstitute dried tomatoes, place them in a bowl and pour in enough boiling water to cover them. Let them sit for 20 minutes, then drain and pat with paper towels to remove as much water as possible. Don't use oil-packed sun-dried tomatoes for this dish, as they may add too much oil to the dressing.

2 pounds white potatoes
¾ cup coarsely chopped reconstituted sun-dried tomatoes
2 tablespoons capers, drained
1 teaspoon dried basil or 3 teaspoons chopped fresh basil
½ cup mayonnaise
½ cup sour cream
1 teaspoon Dijon mustard
½ teaspoon salt
½ teaspoon freshly ground black pepper
1 tablespoon chopped chives

Place the potatoes in a large pot, add enough water to cover them, cover the pot with a lid, and bring to a boil. Cook until the potatoes are pierced easily with the tip of a sharp knife, 15 to 20 minutes. Drain and let cool until you can handle them but they are still warm. Peel and cut into approximately 1-inch pieces.

In a large bowl, combine the sun-dried tomatoes, capers, basil, mayonnaise, sour cream, Dijon mustard, salt, black pepper, and chives. Stir in the potatoes. Cover and refrigerate for several hours or overnight.

SERVES 6

Parmesan Potato Salad

My friend Carol Reuss in Pittsboro, North Carolina, suggested this combination of ingredients. It's OK to use frozen green beans if fresh aren't available.

- 2 pounds new potatoes
- ¾ cup sour cream
- ¼ cup mayonnaise
- ½ teaspoon chopped garlic
- ¾ cup grated Parmesan cheese
- ½ teaspoon salt
- ½ teaspoon freshly ground black pepper
- 1¼ cups cooked green beans, in 1-inch pieces
- 1 (7.5-ounce) jar marinated artichoke hearts, drained and coarsely chopped
- ½ cup sliced almonds

Place the potatoes in a large pot, add enough water to cover them, cover the pot with a lid, and bring to a boil. Cook until the potatoes are pierced easily with the tip of a sharp knife, 15 to 20 minutes. Drain and let cool until you can handle them but they are still warm. Cut into quarters.

In a large bowl, combine the sour cream, mayonnaise, garlic, Parmesan cheese, salt, and pepper. Stir in the green beans, chopped artichoke hearts, almonds, and potatoes. Cover and refrigerate for several hours or overnight.

SERVES 6

Hungarian Potatoes

My friend Liz Biro in Fayetteville, North Carolina, says her father enjoys making potatoes as a side dish. I made a few additions to his recipe and turned it into an unusual potato salad. Hungarian paprika is sweeter and more flavorful than the kind you use to garnish deviled eggs. It's worth seeking out for this dish.

2 pounds Yukon Gold potatoes
4 strips bacon, coarsely chopped
1 cup chopped onion
¼ cup chopped green bell pepper
½ teaspoon chopped garlic
1½ tablespoons Hungarian paprika
1 tablespoon apple cider vinegar
1 teaspoon dill pickle relish

Place the potatoes in a large pot, add enough water to cover them, cover the pot with a lid, and bring to a boil. Cook until the potatoes are pierced easily with the tip of a sharp knife, 15 to 20 minutes. Drain and let cool until you can handle them. Peel and cut into 1- to 1½-inch cubes.

In a large sauté pan over medium heat, cook the bacon, stirring occasionally, until it is brown. Remove the bacon from the pan and drain on paper towels. Add the onion, bell pepper, and garlic to the pan. Cook, stirring, until the vegetables are soft but not browned, 5 to 6 minutes. Adjust the heat if necessary to prevent browning. Stir in the potatoes and toss for a few seconds to combine everything.

Remove the pan from the heat. Stir in the paprika, vinegar, and relish. Place the salad in a large bowl, let cool to room temperature, and serve, or cover and refrigerate overnight. Bring to room temperature to serve.

SERVES 6

Greek Potato Salad

This salad is tart and creamy, with the bite of feta cheese. A Greek friend said this was "just like Mom makes."

- 2 pounds Yukon Gold potatoes
- ⅓ cup olive oil
- 2 tablespoons white wine vinegar
- ½ teaspoon dried oregano or 1½ teaspoons chopped fresh oregano
- ½ cup chopped fresh Italian parsley
- ⅓ cup pitted, chopped Kalamata olives
- ¼ cup chopped celery
- ¼ cup chopped onion
- ½ teaspoon salt
- ½ teaspoon freshly ground black pepper
- ¾ cup crumbled feta cheese

Place the potatoes in a large pot, add enough water to cover them, cover the pot with a lid, and bring to a boil. Cook until the potatoes are pierced easily with the tip of a sharp knife, 15 to 20 minutes. Drain and let cool until you can handle them but they are still warm. Peel and cut into 1- to 1½-inch chunks.

In a large bowl, stir together the olive oil, white wine vinegar, oregano, parsley, olives, celery, onion, salt, and black pepper. Whisk until well combined. Add the potatoes and feta cheese and toss to combine. Cover and let sit at room temperature 2 or 3 hours, or refrigerate for several hours to overnight. Serve at room temperature.

SERVES 6

Blue Moon

I think purple potatoes are a ton of fun, and they retain their vivid color after cooking. They contain the same powerful antioxidant that gives blueberries their color. The crunch of walnuts and the creaminess of the blue cheese are a perfect match in this salad. You can use conventional new potatoes if you can't find purple ones, but you'll miss the eye-catching color. You'll definitely want this salad more than once in a blue moon!

2 pounds purple potatoes
½ cup crumbled blue cheese
¼ cup chopped fresh chives
½ cup coarsely chopped walnuts
¾ cup sour cream
¼ cup mayonnaise
½ teaspoon salt
½ teaspoon freshly ground black pepper
½ cup chopped celery
¼ cup chopped onion

Place the potatoes in a large pot, add enough water to cover them, cover the pot with a lid, and bring to a boil. Cook until the potatoes are pierced easily with the tip of a sharp knife, 10 to 12 minutes. Drain and let cool until you can handle them. Cut them into quarters or halves, depending on the size of the potatoes.

In a large bowl, combine the blue cheese, chives, walnuts, sour cream, mayonnaise, salt, pepper, celery, and onion. Add the potatoes and toss to combine. Cover and refrigerate for several hours to overnight.

SERVES 6

Ruddy Roasted Pepper Salad

The rich flavor of roasted red bell peppers dominates this dish, which will taste best at room temperature. Be sure to chop the peppers finely so that they will blend with the other ingredients.

- 2 pounds Yukon Gold potatoes
- 1 (12-ounce) jar roasted red bell peppers, drained and finely chopped
- ¾ teaspoon chopped garlic
- ¼ cup chopped onion
- 2 tablespoons lemon juice
- ¼ cup olive oil
- ½ teaspoon dried thyme or 1½ teaspoons chopped fresh thyme
- ½ teaspoon dried oregano or 1½ teaspoons chopped fresh oregano
- ¾ teaspoon salt
- ½ teaspoon freshly ground black pepper

Place the potatoes in a large pot, add enough water to cover them, cover the pot with a lid, and bring to a boil. Cook until the potatoes are pierced easily with the tip of a sharp knife, 15 to 20 minutes. Drain and let cool until you can handle them. Peel and cut into 1- to 1½-inch pieces.

In a large bowl, combine the roasted red bell peppers, garlic, onion, lemon juice, olive oil, thyme, oregano, salt, and pepper. Stir in the potatoes. Cover and let sit at room temperature 2 hours or refrigerate overnight. Serve at room temperature.

SERVES 6

Caesar Potato Salad

My neighbor, Cathy Hedberg, makes this recipe frequently because it is a big hit with her family. All I have to say is hail, Caesar!

2 pounds new potatoes
8 cloves garlic, unpeeled
¼ teaspoon salt
¼ teaspoon freshly ground black pepper
1 tablespoon fresh lemon juice
1½ tablespoons olive oil
2 teaspoons anchovy paste
⅓ cup diced red onion
¼ cup chopped fresh Italian parsley
2 tablespoons Parmesan cheese

Place the potatoes and the garlic cloves in a large pot, add enough water to cover them, cover the pot with a lid, and bring to a boil. Cook until the potatoes are pierced easily with the tip of a sharp knife, 15 to 20 minutes. Drain and let cool until you can handle them. Cut the potatoes into quarters.

Peel the garlic, put it in a large bowl, and mash the cloves. Stir and mash in the salt, pepper, lemon juice, olive oil, anchovy paste, and 1 tablespoon of water. Add the potatoes, onion, parsley, and Parmesan cheese, and toss. Serve warm or cover and chill.

SERVES 6

Sweet Potato Salad with Orange-Poppy Seed Dressing

A bit of sweet and a bit of crunch make a potato salad with a lot of personality. If you make this dish ahead and refrigerate it, don't serve it cold, but at room temperature.

2 pounds sweet potatoes
1 cup chopped celery
½ cup cooked green peas
¼ cup golden raisins
2 tablespoons vegetable oil
¼ cup white wine vinegar
2 teaspoons sugar
½ teaspoon salt
½ teaspoon freshly ground black pepper
6 tablespoons fresh orange juice
½ teaspoon fresh lime juice
2 teaspoons poppy seeds

Place the potatoes in a large pot, add enough water to cover them, cover the pot with a lid, and bring to a boil. Cook until the potatoes are pierced easily with the tip of a sharp knife, 15 to 20 minutes. Drain and let cool until you can handle them. Peel and cut into 1- to 1½-inch chunks.

In a large bowl, toss the potatoes with the celery, peas, and raisins. In a small bowl, whisk together the oil, vinegar, sugar, salt, pepper, orange juice, lime juice, and poppy seeds. Pour the dressing over the vegetables and toss to coat. Cover and let sit 2 hours or refrigerate overnight.

SERVES 4

Beet and Potato Salad

Linda Naylor, a great cook in Chapel Hill, North Carolina, sent me this favorite recipe that includes another root vegetable along with the potatoes. She got the recipe at an area farmers market several years ago.

¾ pound beets
¾ pound potatoes
California Dressing (recipe follows)

Place the beets and potatoes in separate pots, add enough water to cover, cover with lids, and bring to a boil. Cook until easily pierced with a sharp knife, 15 to 30 minutes, depending on the size of the beets and potatoes. Cool both until you can handle them. Peel and cut into small pieces.

Place the beets and potatoes in a large bowl, pour the California Dressing over them, and toss to coat.

MAKES ABOUT 1 CUP

California Dressing

½ cup mayonnaise
2 tablespoons ketchup
1 teaspoon minced scallions
1 teaspoon minced garlic
1 tablespoon minced fresh bronze fennel fronds or other fresh herb of your choice
Salt and pepper to taste

Stir together the mayonnaise, ketchup, scallions, garlic, and herbs. Taste, then add salt and pepper. Store, covered, in the refrigerator.

SERVES 4 TO 6

Less-Dressed Potato Salad with Fennel and Chives

This sophisticated salad is lightly dressed in a simple lemony vinaigrette to let the flavors of the potatoes and fennel come though. As a variation, add some cooked green beans cut into 1-inch pieces. Excerpted from *Vegan Planet,* by Robin Robertson (Harvard Common Press, 2003).

1½ pounds small red potatoes
½ cup minced fennel bulb
¼ cup niçoise olives, pitted
¼ cup chopped fresh chives
⅓ cup extra virgin olive oil
2 tablespoons fresh lemon juice
1 teaspoon Dijon mustard
1 shallot, minced
Salt and freshly ground black pepper

Place the potatoes in a large saucepan with salted water to cover. Bring to a boil over medium-high heat and continue to boil until tender, about 30 minutes. Drain and cut into halves or quarters, depending on the size of the potatoes. Transfer to a large serving bowl and add the fennel, olives, and chives. Set aside.

In a small bowl, whisk together the olive oil, lemon juice, mustard, and shallot, and toss gently to combine. Taste and adjust the seasonings. Serve right away or cover tightly and refrigerate until ready to serve. This will keep for 2 to 3 days.

SERVES 6

Wasabi Spuds

The fiery green Japanese horseradish wasabi has moved from the sushi bar to the home pantry in the form of sauces and dressing. This potato salad will have 'em talking at the potluck. I used wasabi sauce, found in the Asian section of the supermarket, but wasabi mayonnaise would work, too, although the wasabi flavor might not be as strong.

2 pounds new potatoes
½ cup wasabi sauce
¼ teaspoon soy sauce
1 cup canned sliced water chestnuts, drained
¼ cup chopped onion
¼ cup sliced almonds

Place the potatoes in a large pot, add enough water to cover them, cover the pot with a lid, and bring to a boil. Cook until the potatoes are pierced easily with the tip of a sharp knife, 15 to 20 minutes. Drain and let cool until you can handle them. Cut into quarters or halves, depending on the size of the potatoes.

In a large bowl, combine the wasabi sauce, soy sauce, water chestnuts, onion, almonds, and potatoes. Cover and refrigerate for several hours or overnight.

SERVES 6

Grilled Sweet Potato Salad with Chipotle Vinaigrette

The smoky sweetness of grilled sweet potatoes and the smoky heat of chipotles make this an unusual potato salad. Use a perforated grill pan, available at kitchen stores, to prevent the slices from falling through the grill. Here's a tip: If some slices aren't quite done when you take them off the grill but you're afraid of burning them with further grilling, pop them in the microwave for 15 to 30 seconds to complete the cooking.

- ¼ cup fresh orange juice
- 1 canned chipotle in adobo sauce plus ½ teaspoon of adobo sauce
- ⅓ cup olive oil
- ¼ teaspoon fresh lime juice
- ½ teaspoon chopped garlic
- ½ teaspoon salt
- 2 pounds sweet potatoes, peeled and cut into ½-inch slices
- ¾ cup chopped red onion
- 2 tablespoons chopped fresh cilantro

Place the orange juice, chipotle, adobo sauce, olive oil, lime juice, garlic, and salt in a food processor or blender. Process for a few minutes, until the chipotle is pureed and the mixture is smooth. Set aside.

Prepare a gas or charcoal grill for direct cooking at medium heat. Spray the grill or grill pan with nonstick cooking spray before heating it. Place the slices of sweet potato on the grill and cook for 20 to 30 minutes, turning frequently, until the slices are tender when pierced with the tip of a sharp knife.

Place the potatoes and onion in a large bowl. Pour in the chipotle vinaigrette and toss to coat. Add the cilantro and gently toss. Let sit 30 minutes and serve, or cover and refrigerate overnight, then bring to room temperature before serving.

SERVES 6

Tarragon-Lemon Potato Salad

I've always thought of tarragon as an elegant herb. Maybe that's because it's used so widely in French cooking. The aniselike flavor is strong, but goes well with the lilt of lemon.

2 pounds new potatoes
½ cup chopped celery
⅓ cup chopped fresh Italian parsley
½ cup sour cream
¾ teaspoon chopped garlic
¾ teaspoon grated lemon zest
1 teaspoon fresh lemon juice
2 tablespoons dill pickle relish
1½ teaspoons dried tarragon or 4¼ teaspoons chopped fresh tarragon
¾ teaspoon salt
¾ teaspoon freshly ground black pepper

Place the potatoes in a large pot, add enough water to cover them, cover the pot with a lid, and bring to a boil. Cook until the potatoes are pierced easily with the tip of a sharp knife, 15 to 20 minutes. Drain and let cool until you can handle them. Cut into quarters or halves, depending on the size of the potatoes.

In a large bowl, toss together the potatoes, celery, and parsley. In a small bowl, stir together the sour cream, garlic, lemon zest, lemon juice, dill pickle relish, tarragon, salt, and pepper. Pour the dressing over the vegetables and toss to coat. Cover and refrigerate for several hours or overnight.

SERVES 6

Sweet Potatoes with Lime Vinaigrette

Sweet and tangy—don't you love it? Serrano chiles are medium-hot, but still take care in chopping them. Wash your hands thoroughly afterwards. If you can't find serranos, fresh jalapeños would work well, too.

2 pounds sweet potatoes
1 cup sliced red onion, slices cut into half-moons
¼ cup plus 1 tablespoon fresh lime juice
1 teaspoon grated lime zest
½ cup olive oil
½ teaspoon salt
½ teaspoon freshly ground black pepper
½ teaspoon sugar
½ teaspoon chopped garlic
½ fresh serrano chile, seeded and finely chopped

Place the potatoes in a large pot, add enough water to cover them, cover the pot with a lid, and bring to a boil. Cook until the potatoes are pierced easily with the tip of a sharp knife, 15 to 20 minutes. The cooking time will depend on the size of the potatoes. Drain and let cool until you can handle them. Peel and cut into ½-inch slices, then cut the slices in half.

In a large bowl, toss together the potatoes and red onion. In a small bowl, whisk together the lime juice, lime zest, olive oil, salt, pepper, sugar, garlic, and serrano chile. Pour the dressing over the vegetables and toss to coat. Cover and let sit at room temperature for 1 hour and serve, or refrigerate for several hours to overnight. Serve at room temperature.

SERVES 8

Red, White, and Blue Potato Salad

Serve this colorful salad as a surprise addition to the Fourth of July picnic. Since the colors are important, don't substitute other potato varieties for the ones specified. The recipe comes courtesy of the United States Potato Board.

1 pound small white potatoes (creamer fingerling or Yukon Gold)
1 pound small red potatoes
12 ounces purple Peruvian potatoes
3 tablespoons walnut oil or olive oil, divided in three parts
2 ounces chopped ham
⅓ cup chopped walnuts
8 garlic cloves, finely chopped
3 tablespoons sherry or white balsamic vinegar
1 cup finely chopped red or orange bell pepper
4 scallions, chopped
½ teaspoon salt
¼ teaspoon freshly ground black pepper

Cut the potatoes into 1 ½-inch pieces (do not peel). Steam for 25 minutes or until potatoes are tender.

Heat 1 tablespoon of the walnut or olive oil in a medium skillet. Add the ham, walnuts, and garlic and cook, stirring, for 10 minutes. Add the vinegar and stir well. In a large bowl, toss ham mixture with potatoes, remaining 2 tablespoons of oil, bell pepper, scallions, salt, and pepper. Serve warm or cold.

SERVES 6

Asian Roots

Edamame—fresh soybeans—are popular snacks at sushi bars. They're widely available in supermarket freezer cases, so it's easy to give a potato salad an Asian twist. Feel free to substitute regular radishes if you can't find daikon.

2 pounds new potatoes
1 cup shelled edamame
¾ cup peeled and chopped daikon radish
1 tablespoon chopped garlic
⅔ cup vegetable oil
2½ teaspoons soy sauce
¼ cup white wine vinegar or rice vinegar

Place the potatoes in a large pot, add enough water to cover them, cover the pot with a lid, and bring to a boil. Cook until the potatoes are pierced easily with the tip of a sharp knife, 15 to 20 minutes. Drain and let cool until you can handle them. Cut into quarters or halves, depending on the size of the potatoes.

In a large bowl, toss together the potatoes, edamame, and daikon. In a small bowl, whisk together the garlic, oil, soy sauce, and vinegar. Pour the dressing over the vegetables and toss to coat. Cover and let sit at room temperature 2 hours and serve, or refrigerate for several hours to overnight. Serve at room temperature.

SERVES 8

Rick's Potatoes

My book club friend Sarah Pearson in Raleigh, North Carolina, says this recipe with the fresh flavor of mint is addictive. "We call it Rick's Potatoes, since we got it from my husband's brother," she says.

5½ pounds small new potatoes
8 cloves garlic, minced
1½ cups olive oil
1 large or 2 small bunches fresh mint, finely chopped
2 tablespoons salt
Freshly ground black pepper to taste

Preheat the oven to 350°F. Scrub the potatoes and prick each one 6 times with a fork. Place the potatoes in a shallow roasting pan and roast for 2 hours or until easily pierced with a sharp knife. When done, cut each potato in half.

In a large bowl, combine the garlic, olive oil, mint, and salt. Taste, then add pepper. Add the potatoes and toss to combine. Cover and let stand for 30 minutes, then serve or refrigerate for up to two days. Bring to room temperature to serve.

SERVES 6

Prosciutto and Parmesan Salad

Italian prosciutto adds a sophisticated flavor to these spuds. They would be great with some grilled chicken flavored with oregano or other Italian herbs.

- 2 pounds new potatoes
- 3 ounces prosciutto, coarsely shredded
- ¾ cup cooked green beans, cut into 1-inch pieces
- 2 tablespoons chopped fresh Italian parsley
- 2 tablespoons chopped fresh chives
- 1 tablespoon grated Parmesan cheese
- 1 tablespoon chopped garlic
- ¾ cup sour cream
- ¾ teaspoon Dijon mustard
- 2 teaspoons fresh lemon juice
- 1 teaspoon salt
- 1 teaspoon freshly ground black pepper

Place the potatoes in a large pot, add enough water to cover them, cover the pot with a lid, and bring to a boil. Cook until the potatoes are pierced easily with the tip of a sharp knife, 15 to 20 minutes. Drain and let cool until you can handle them. Cut into quarters or halves, depending on the size of the potatoes.

In a large bowl, toss together the potatoes, prosciutto, green beans, parsley, and chives. In a small bowl, stir together the Parmesan cheese, garlic, sour cream, Dijon mustard, lemon juice, salt, and black pepper. Pour the dressing over the vegetables and toss to coat. Cover and refrigerate for several hours to overnight.

SERVES 6

Spuds Step Out

Wow your guests with this elegant, rich salad that includes salmon caviar. The pink pearls look beautiful scattered among the other ingredients, so be careful not to mash too many of them while stirring the salad together. Use at least 3 ounces of the caviar, but feel free to add more to your own preference.

- 2 pounds new potatoes
- 3 hard-cooked large eggs, chopped
- 1 tablespoon chopped fresh Italian parsley
- 2 teaspoons chopped fresh chives
- ¾ cup sour cream
- ¾ teaspoon Dijon mustard
- 1 teaspoon fresh lemon juice
- ½ teaspoon Worcestershire sauce
- ¼ teaspoon salt
- 3 to 4 ounces salmon caviar

Place the potatoes in a large pot, add enough water to cover them, cover the pot with a lid, and bring to a boil. Cook until the potatoes are pierced easily with the tip of a sharp knife, 15 to 20 minutes. Drain and let cool until you can handle them. Cut into small pieces; at least quarters or halves, depending on the size of the potatoes.

In a large bowl, toss together the potatoes, eggs, parsley, and chives. In a small bowl, stir together the sour cream, Dijon mustard, lemon juice, Worcestershire sauce, and salt. Pour the dressing over the vegetables and toss to coat. Gently stir in the caviar. Cover and refrigerate for several hours to overnight.

SPUD SUPPERS

SERVES 6

Potato Salad Niçoise-Style

I drew inspiration from the traditional French *salade niçoise* for this recipe, but I used easy-to-find canned tuna. Grilled fresh tuna would be even better.

2 pounds small red potatoes
¼ pound green beans
¼ cup chopped red onion
2 tablespoons chopped pitted Kalamata olives
2 hard-cooked large eggs, coarsely chopped
¾ cup canned white tuna in water, drained and flaked
¾ cup olive oil
3 tablespoons red wine vinegar
½ teaspoon chopped garlic
3 teaspoons Dijon mustard
¾ teaspoon salt
¾ teaspoon freshly ground black pepper
¼ cup chopped fresh Italian parsley

Place the potatoes in a large pot, add enough water to cover them, cover the pot with a lid, and bring to a boil. Cook until the potatoes are pierced easily with the tip of a sharp knife, 15 to 20 minutes. Drain and let cool until you can handle them but they are still warm.

Break the green beans in approximately 1-inch pieces and steam until just done but still bright green, just a couple of minutes in the microwave.

Cut the potatoes into chunks of similar size, either into quarters or eighths, depending on the size of the potatoes.

Place the potatoes in a large bowl. Add the green beans, red onion, olives, eggs, and tuna. Toss lightly.

continues on p. 104

In a small bowl, whisk together the olive oil, vinegar, garlic, mustard, salt, and pepper. Pour the mixture over the potato mixture and toss to combine. Cover and refrigerate for several hours to overnight. When ready to serve, garnish with the parsley.

SERVES 6

Brunch-Time Potato Salad

This salad was inspired by breakfast casseroles, which make great centerpieces for brunch. The advantage of a potato salad is that it can be made ahead and is ready to go when you're ready to eat.

- 2 pounds white potatoes
- ⅔ cup grated cheddar cheese
- ½ cup crumbled cooked bacon
- 2 hard-cooked large eggs, chopped
- ¼ cup chopped red onion
- 1¼ cups mayonnaise
- ½ teaspoon salt, or to taste
- ½ teaspoon freshly ground black pepper, or to taste
- ¼ cup chopped fresh Italian parsley

Place the potatoes in a large pot, add enough water to cover them, cover the pot with a lid, and bring to a boil. Cook until the potatoes are pierced easily with the tip of a sharp knife, 15 to 20 minutes. Drain and let cool until you can handle them but they are still warm. Peel and cut into approximately 1-inch pieces.

In a large bowl, combine the cheddar cheese, bacon, eggs, red onion, mayonnaise, salt, black pepper, and parsley. Stir in the potatoes. Cover and refrigerate for several hours to overnight.

SERVES 6

Dilly Shrimp Salad

A potato salad for seafood lovers! And they said it couldn't be done... Save time by purchasing cooked shrimp at the supermarket seafood counter, or use frozen cooked shrimp.

2 pounds new potatoes
1 cup sour cream
½ cup chopped scallions
3 tablespoons chopped fresh dill
2 teaspoons fresh lemon juice
½ cup chopped red bell pepper
½ teaspoon salt
½ teaspoon freshly ground black pepper
¾ pound cooked shrimp, deveined and shells and tails removed

Place the potatoes in a large pot, add enough water to cover them, cover the pot with a lid, and bring to a boil. Cook until the potatoes are pierced easily with the tip of a sharp knife, 15 to 20 minutes. Drain and let cool until you can handle them but they are still warm. Cut them into quarters.

In a large bowl, combine the sour cream, scallions, dill, lemon juice, red bell pepper, salt, and black pepper.

Cut the shrimp in half, then add to the dressing mixture. Add the potatoes and stir well. Cover and refrigerate for several hours to overnight.

SERVES 6

Very Veggie Salad

"Why do Southerners put bacon in everything?" asked my husband's coworker Steve, a vegetarian. Well, Steve, because it's *good.* But to show him that Southerners eat vegetables, too, here's a salad packed with veggies. It's hearty and pretty enough to star at lunch or dinner—even without bacon.

2 pounds Yukon Gold potatoes
½ cup cooked green peas
½ cup chopped celery
⅔ cup grated carrots
½ cup chopped red bell pepper
2 hard-cooked large eggs, chopped
½ cup chopped scallions
½ cup sour cream
¼ cup mayonnaise
1 tablespoon chopped fresh chives
2 teaspoons fresh lemon juice
1 teaspoon Dijon mustard
¾ teaspoon salt
¾ teaspoon freshly ground black pepper

Place the potatoes in a large pot, add enough water to cover them, cover the pot with a lid, and bring to a boil. Cook until the potatoes are pierced easily with the tip of a sharp knife, 15 to 20 minutes. Drain and let cool until you can handle them. Peel and cut into 1- to 1½-inch chunks. Let cool to room temperature while you prepare the other ingredients.

In a large bowl, combine the peas, celery, carrots, red bell pepper, eggs, and scallions. In a separate small bowl, stir together the sour cream, mayonnaise, chives, lemon juice, Dijon mustard, salt, and black pepper.

Add the potatoes to the vegetables and toss to combine. Pour on the sour cream mixture and stir to coat the vegetables. Cover and refrigerate for several hours to overnight.

SERVES 6

Smoked Salmon Salad

Smoked salmon lovers, this one's for you! The tang of the capers and onion balance the fish's rich flavor. Creole mustard contains horseradish, which also adds a little bite.

- 2 pounds new potatoes
- 1½ cups sour cream
- ¾ teaspoon Creole mustard
- 3 teaspoons fresh lemon juice
- ¾ teaspoon salt
- ¾ teaspoon freshly ground black pepper
- ½ cup chopped red onion
- 2 tablespoons drained capers
- ¾ cup chopped smoked salmon
- 1 hard-cooked large egg, chopped

Place the potatoes in a large pot, add enough water to cover them, cover the pot with a lid, and bring to a boil. Cook until the potatoes are pierced easily with the tip of a sharp knife, 15 to 20 minutes. Drain and let cool until you can handle them. Cut into quarters.

In a large bowl, combine the sour cream, Creole mustard, lemon juice, salt, and black pepper. Stir in the onion, capers, smoked salmon, and egg. Add the potatoes and stir well. Cover and refrigerate for several hours to overnight.

SERVES 6

Buffalo Chicken Spuds

Spicy Buffalo chicken wings are a favorite snack. When you combine the flavor with potato salad, you get a hearty salad that will fill up wings fans.

- 2 pounds Yukon Gold potatoes
- 1½ cups cooked, shredded chicken
- 1 cup chopped celery
- ½ cup chopped red onion
- 2 tablespoons hot pepper sauce (such as Tabasco)
- ⅔ cup vegetable oil
- 1 teaspoon chopped garlic
- 1 teaspoon salt
- 1 teaspoon freshly ground black pepper
- 1 teaspoon apple cider vinegar
- ¼ teaspoon sugar
- Celery leaves for garnish (optional)

Place the potatoes in a large pot, add enough water to cover them, cover the pot with a lid, and bring to a boil. Cook until the potatoes are pierced easily with the tip of a sharp knife, 15 to 20 minutes. Drain and let cool until you can handle them. Peel the potatoes and cut into 1- to 1½-inch pieces.

In a large bowl, toss together the potatoes, chicken, celery, and onion. In a separate small bowl, whisk together the hot pepper sauce, oil, garlic, salt, black pepper, vinegar, and sugar. Pour the dressing over the vegetables and toss to coat. Cover and let sit at room temperature 2 hours or refrigerate overnight. Let come to room temperature before serving. When ready to serve, garnish with a few celery leaves, if desired.

SERVES 6 TO 8

Potato Salad with Crab

Chef Stephanie Tyson loves sweet potatoes so much that she named her restaurant in Winston-Salem, North Carolina, after them. Sweet Potatoes serves great twists on Southern classics. This recipe uses white potatoes, which shows that the chef can do great things with them, too.

2 quarts (8 cups) cooked and diced white potatoes (about 3 pounds raw potatoes)
¾ cup diced onion
½ cup diced celery
¼ cup diced pimientos
1 teaspoon salt
1 teaspoon freshly ground black pepper
1 cup Dressing (recipe follows)
½ pound cooked lump crabmeat

In a large bowl, combine the potatoes, onion, celery, pimientos, salt, pepper, and Dressing. Cover and let sit about 2 hours. When ready to serve, top with the crabmeat.

MAKES ABOUT 1 CUP

Dressing

3 tablespoons fresh lemon juice
1 tablespoon grated lemon zest
2 tablespoons white vinegar
2 tablespoons Dijon mustard
1 teaspoon chopped garlic
2 tablespoons dried tarragon
1 teaspoon fresh dill
1 tablespoon sugar
1½ cups olive oil

In a small bowl, combine the lemon juice, lemon zest, white vinegar, Dijon mustard, garlic, tarragon, dill, and sugar. Slowly whisk in the olive oil.

SERVES 6

Picnic Salad

Everyone loves potato salad and chicken salad on a picnic, right? Well, why not combine both in one bowl! It's a great way to use leftover roasted chicken. If you don't have leftovers, use one 9.75-ounce can of cooked white-meat chicken.

2 pounds new potatoes
¾ cup mayonnaise
½ teaspoon salt
½ teaspoon freshly ground black pepper
1 teaspoon fresh lemon juice
2 tablespoons sweet pickle relish
½ cup chopped celery
½ cup chopped onion
1½ cups chopped cooked chicken

Place the potatoes in a large pot, add enough water to cover them, cover the pot with a lid, and bring to a boil. Cook until the potatoes are pierced easily with the tip of a sharp knife, 15 to 20 minutes. Drain and let cool until you can handle them. Cut into quarters or halves, depending on the size of the potatoes.

In a large bowl, combine the mayonnaise, salt, pepper, lemon juice, and pickle relish. Stir in the celery, onion, and chicken, then stir in the potatoes. Toss to coat all the ingredients. Cover and refrigerate for several hours to overnight.

SERVES 6

Pizza Potatoes

The beloved pizzeria flavors of pepperoni and Parmesan taste great in potato salad, too. Put some toasted garlic bread and a leafy green salad alongside this one, and you have lunch.

- 2 pounds Yukon Gold potatoes
- 1¼ cups sour cream
- 3 teaspoons Dijon mustard
- ¾ teaspoon salt
- ¾ teaspoon freshly ground black pepper
- ½ cup chopped green bell pepper
- ½ cup chopped red onion
- 4 tablespoons grated Parmesan cheese
- 1½ cups coarsely chopped pepperoni
- Fresh oregano leaves for garnish (optional)

Place the potatoes in a large pot, add enough water to cover them, cover the pot with a lid, and bring to a boil. Cook until the potatoes are pierced easily with the tip of a sharp knife, 15 to 20 minutes. Drain and let cool until you can handle them. Peel and cut into 1- to 1½-inch pieces.

In a large bowl, combine the sour cream, mustard, salt, and pepper. Stir in the bell pepper, onion, Parmesan cheese, pepperoni, and potatoes. Cover and refrigerate for several hours to overnight. When ready to serve, garnish with a few fresh oregano leaves, if desired.

SERVES 6

Spring Ham Salad

"What a great way to use up that leftover Easter ham!" said one of my pork-loving tasters. The colors in this salad will remind you of a fresh spring day.

2 pounds new potatoes
1½ cups cubed cooked ham
½ cup cooked peas
2 hard-cooked large eggs, chopped
2 tablespoons sweet pickle relish, with juice
½ cup chopped fresh Italian parsley
1½ cups mayonnaise
1½ teaspoons yellow mustard
⅓ cup chopped onion
¾ teaspoon salt
¾ teaspoon freshly ground black pepper

Place the potatoes in a large pot, add enough water to cover them, cover the pot with a lid, and bring to a boil. Cook until the potatoes are pierced easily with the tip of a sharp knife, 15 to 20 minutes. Drain and let cool until you can handle them. Cut into quarters or halves, depending on the size of the potatoes.

In a large bowl, combine the ham, peas, eggs, relish, parsley, mayonnaise, mustard, onion, salt, and pepper. Stir in the potatoes. Cover and refrigerate for several hours to overnight.

SERVES 6

Carolina BBQ Potato Salad

In North Carolina, barbecue is a noun, not a verb involving your backyard and a grill. And we like our pork barbecue tangy and spicy, using a vinegar sauce with lots of pepper. This salad brings all those great flavors together. Cooked pork barbecue is available at many larger supermarkets. If you can't find it, you could use shredded grilled beef or pork. The vinegar-based barbecue sauce is crucial—don't use a thick, sweet one.

2 pounds new potatoes
1½ cups cooked pork barbecue
½ cup vinegar-based barbecue sauce
⅓ cup chopped onion
½ cup chopped celery
¼ cup chopped fresh Italian parsley

Place the potatoes in a large pot, add enough water to cover them, cover the pot with a lid, and bring to a boil. Cook until the potatoes are pierced easily with the tip of a sharp knife, 15 to 20 minutes. Drain and let cool until you can handle them. Cut into quarters or halves, depending on the size of the potatoes.

In a large bowl, toss together the potatoes, barbecue, barbecue sauce, onion, and celery. Cover and refrigerate for several hours or overnight. Serve at room temperature. When ready to serve, garnish with chopped parsley.

SERVES 6

Potato Salad Cha-Cha-Cha

The Tex-Mex flavors of this recipe will shake up the old family reunion picnic by turning traditional potato salad on its head. The salad is also hearty enough to be the centerpiece of a vegetarian meal. The recipe comes courtesy of the United States Potato Board.

1⅓ pounds (about 4 medium) potatoes, cut into ¾-inch cubes
3 tablespoons vegetable oil
2½ tablespoons fresh lime juice
1½ tablespoons bottled mild jalapeño hot sauce
1½ teaspoons chili powder
½ teaspoon salt (optional)
1 (15-ounce) can black beans, rinsed and drained
1 (7-ounce) can whole kernel corn, drained
1 cup diced tomatoes
½ cup sliced scallions

In a large covered saucepan, cook the potatoes in 2 inches of boiling water until just tender, 10 to 12 minutes. Drain and cool.

Meanwhile, in a large bowl, whisk together the oil, lime juice, jalapeño hot sauce, chili powder, and salt, if desired. Add potatoes and remaining ingredients. Toss gently to mix thoroughly.

SERVES 6

Antipasto Potato Salad

"This is a new type of potato salad for a Southern boy," said one of my tasters. I took the ingredients from the classic Italian antipasto plate. Pepperoncini are pickled Italian peppers that carry some heat.

2 pounds new potatoes
¾ cup matchstick-sliced cooked ham
½ cup matchstick-sliced cooked turkey
½ cup chopped onion
¼ cup chopped pepperoncini
½ cup coarsely chopped pitted black or pimiento-stuffed green olives, or a combination
1½ teaspoons capers
½ cup olive oil
¼ cup white-wine vinegar
½ teaspoon Dijon mustard
½ teaspoon salt
½ teaspoon freshly ground black pepper
2 tablespoons grated Parmesan cheese (optional)

Place the potatoes in a large pot, add enough water to cover them, cover the pot with a lid, and bring to a boil. Cook until the potatoes are pierced easily with the tip of a sharp knife, 15 to 20 minutes.

Drain and let cool until you can handle them. Cut into quarters or halves, depending on the size of the potatoes.

In a large bowl, toss together the ham, turkey, onion, pepperoncini, olives, capers, and potatoes.

In a small bowl, whisk together the olive oil, vinegar, mustard, salt, and pepper. Pour the dressing over the vegetables and toss to coat.

Sprinkle the Parmesan cheese on top, if using. Cover and let sit for about 30 minutes before serving. To serve later, refrigerate overnight before adding the Parmesan, then bring to room temperature and top with Parmesan if desired.

Index

Debbie Moose is a writer and editor whose books include *Wings*, *Deviled Eggs*, and *Fan Fare*. She is a former food editor at the *News & Observer* (Raleigh, North Carolina), where she currently writes two regular columns, "Sunday Dinner" and "The Tasteful Garden."